D0099910

Jun 17

Your Faith

BUDDHISM

By Harriet Brundle

*You can find the **bold** words in this book in the Glossary on page 24.*

PHOTO CREDITS

CONTENTS

©2017
Book Life
King's Lynn
Norfolk PE30 4LS

ISBN: 978-1-78637-034-1

A catalogue record for this book
is available from the British Library.

Written by:
Harriet Brundle

Edited by:
Grace Jones

Designed by:
Natalie Carr

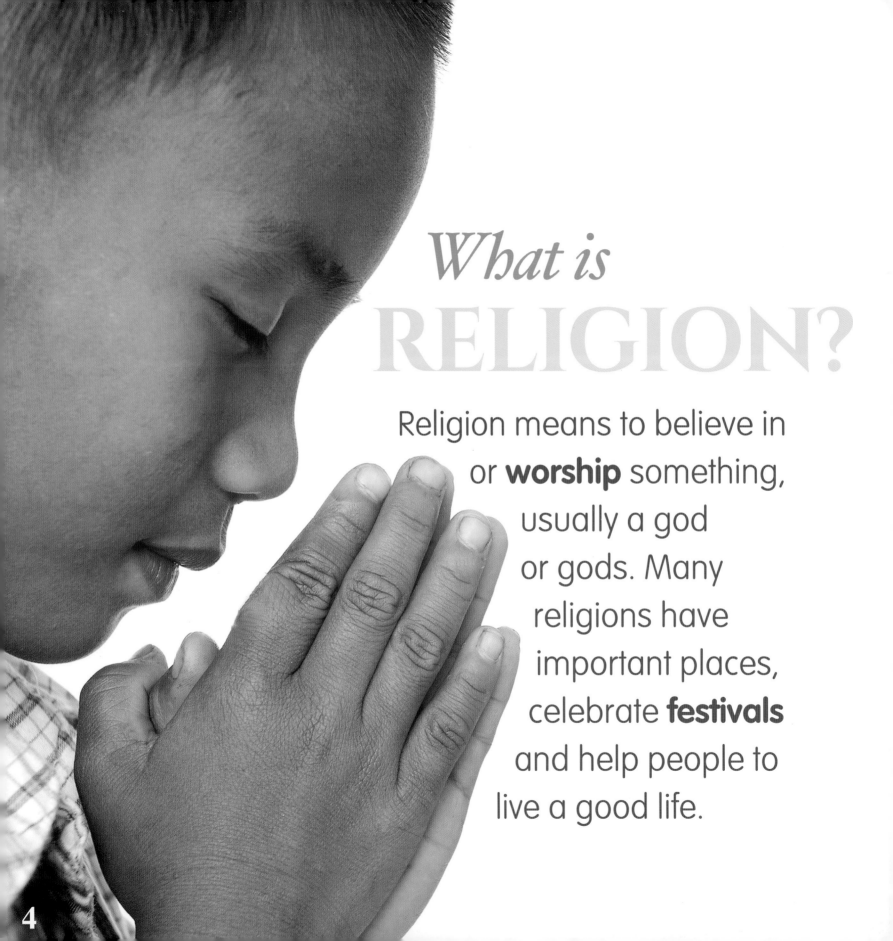

What is RELIGION?

Religion means to believe in or **worship** something, usually a god or gods. Many religions have important places, celebrate **festivals** and help people to live a good life.

4

There are lots of different religions. Other religions with a large amount of followers include Christianity, Islam, Hinduism and Sikhism.

CHRISTIANITY

ISLAM

HINDUISM

SIKHISM

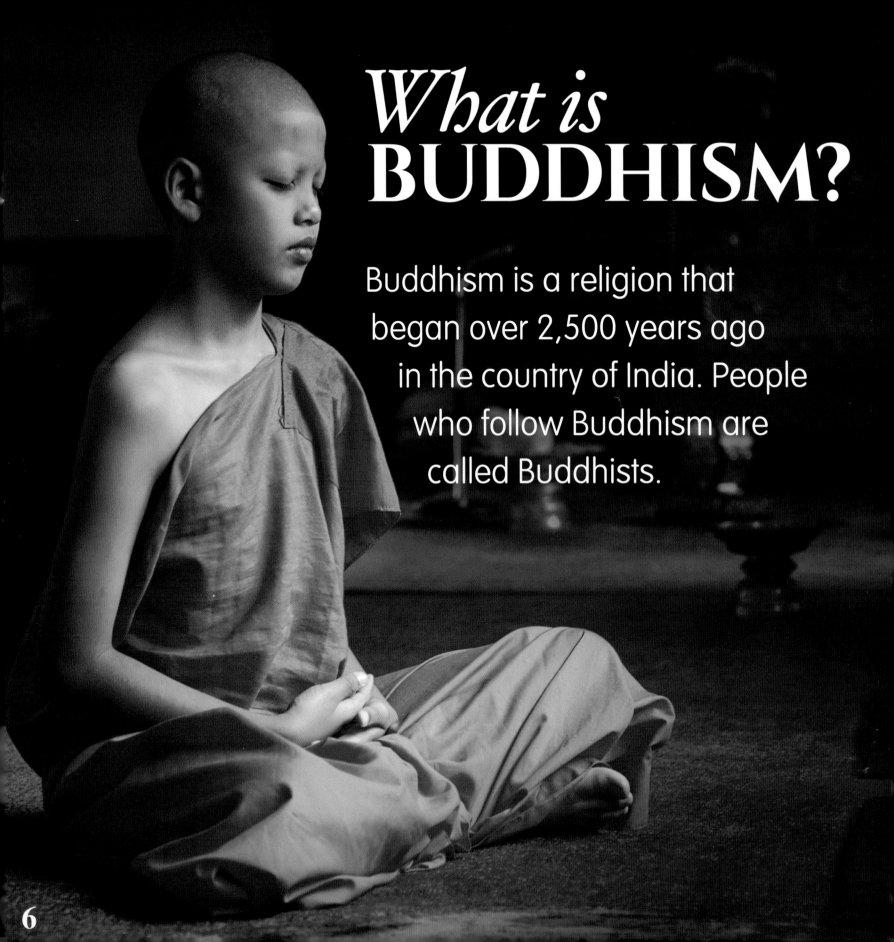

What is BUDDHISM?

Buddhism is a religion that began over 2,500 years ago in the country of India. People who follow Buddhism are called Buddhists.

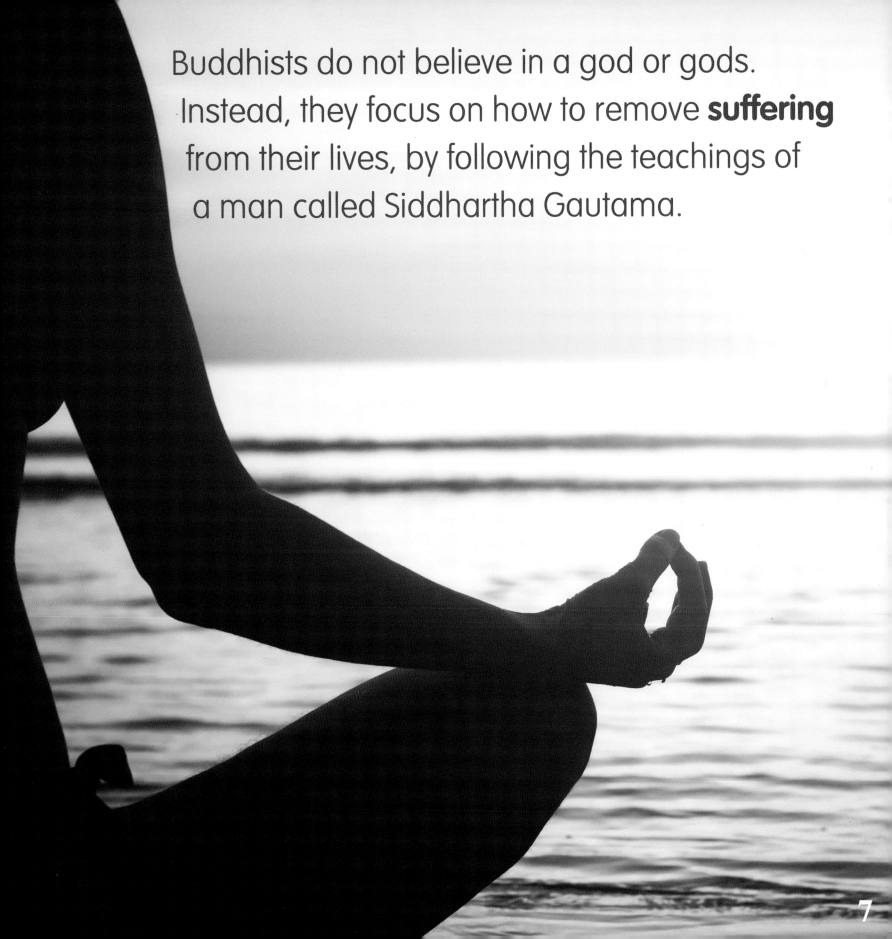

Buddhists do not believe in a god or gods. Instead, they focus on how to remove **suffering** from their lives, by following the teachings of a man called Siddhartha Gautama.

The
BUDDHA

NEPAL

Siddhartha Gautama, also known as Buddha, was born in the country of Nepal thousands of years ago. He was a rich prince who lived a life of wealth and comfort.

One day, he decided to leave his kingdom to go and see the world. He saw people suffering and so he decided to spend his life encouraging others to live a life of balance.

ENLIGHTENMENT

Buddha spent a whole night **meditating** and by the morning he had reached enlightenment. This meant that Buddha was no longer **reborn**.

Reaching enlightenment can also be called nirvana.

After he was enlightened, Buddha spent his life teaching others what he had learned so they could reach enlightenment too.

The TRIPITAKA

The Tripitaka is the earliest known collection of Buddhist teachings. The **contents** of the Tripitaka were decided at the First Buddhist Council, just after the death of Buddha.

The teachings were first written on long, narrow leaves which were grouped into bunches and kept in baskets.

The word 'Tripitaka' means three baskets.

Places of WORSHIP

Buddhists worship at home or at a temple. When worshipping at home, Buddhists will often have a **shrine** with a statue of Buddha and light candles.

When Buddhists worship at a temple, they sit on the floor without any shoes on, facing a picture or a statue of Buddha. They often **chant** and make offerings of flowers and candles.

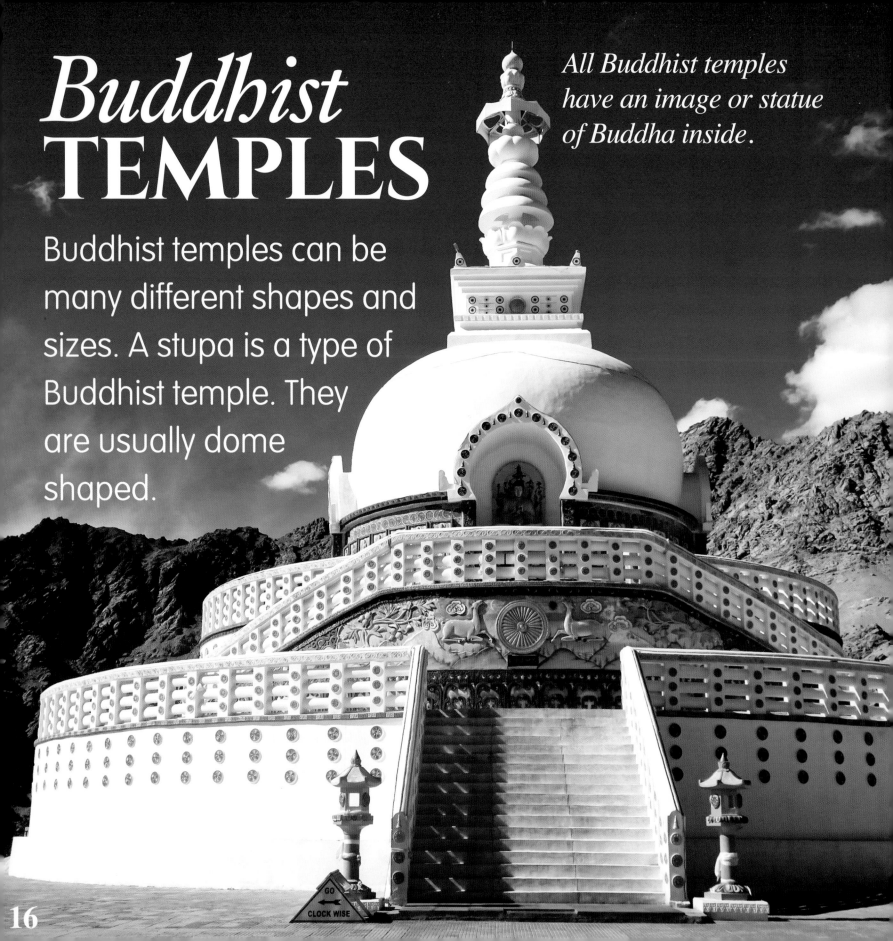

Buddhist TEMPLES

All Buddhist temples have an image or statue of Buddha inside.

Buddhist temples can be many different shapes and sizes. A stupa is a type of Buddhist temple. They are usually dome shaped.

GO CLOCK WISE

16

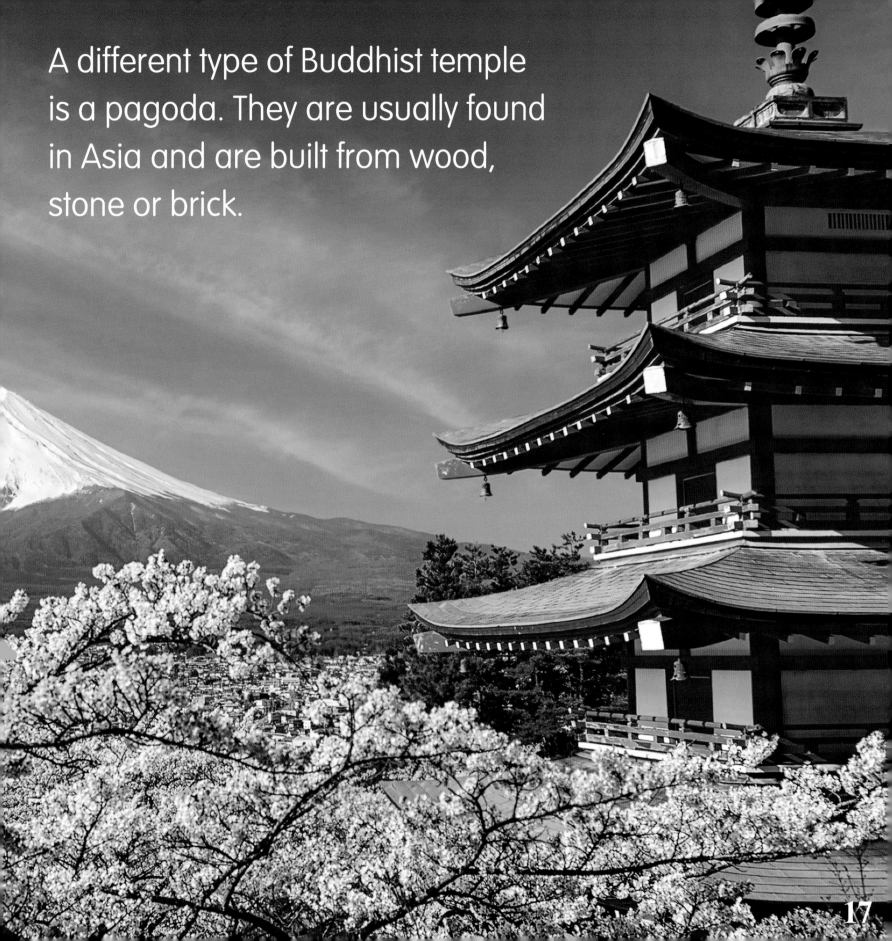

A different type of Buddhist temple is a pagoda. They are usually found in Asia and are built from wood, stone or brick.

The THREE JEWELS

The Three Jewels are three very important Buddhist beliefs. They are:

1. *Belief in Buddha*

2. *The teaching of Buddha (Dharma)*

3. *Helping others to move towards enlightenment*

For Buddhist people, the Three Jewels are at the centre of their daily lives. They believe that the Three Jewels will **shelter** and protect them in the world.

Buddhist FESTIVALS

Celebrations are often very colourful!

The main Buddhist festival is called Buddha Day. Buddhists celebrate Buddha's birth, enlightenment and death by decorating their homes and visiting a temple.

Buddhists around the world also celebrate lots of other important days throughout the year including Buddhist New Year and Dharma Day, a day that celebrates the first time Buddha gave his teachings to others.

Facts About BUDDHISM

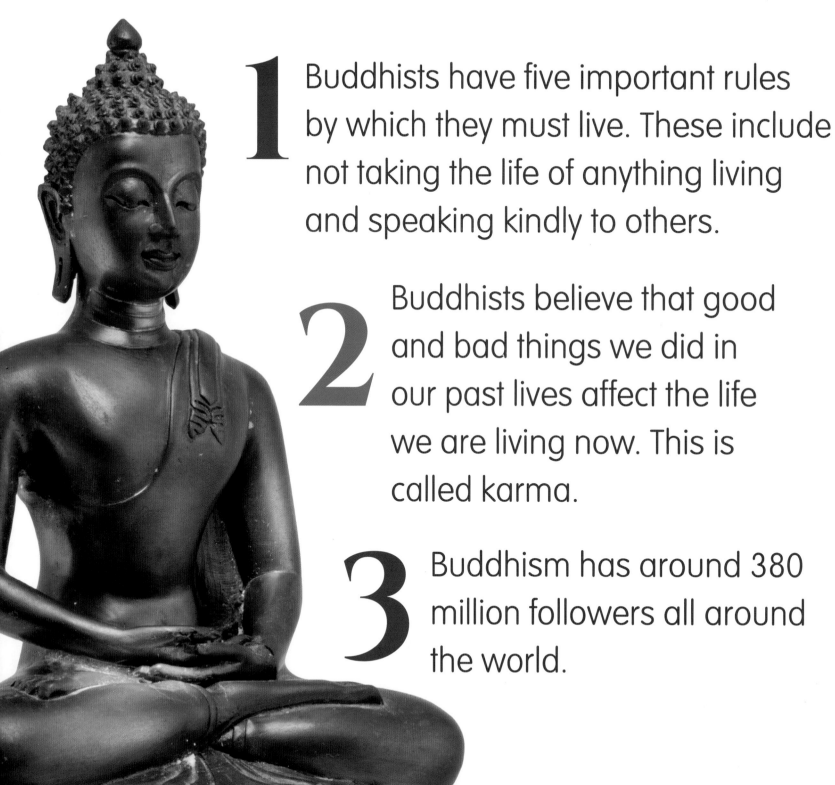

1 Buddhists have five important rules by which they must live. These include not taking the life of anything living and speaking kindly to others.

2 Buddhists believe that good and bad things we did in our past lives affect the life we are living now. This is called karma.

3 Buddhism has around 380 million followers all around the world.

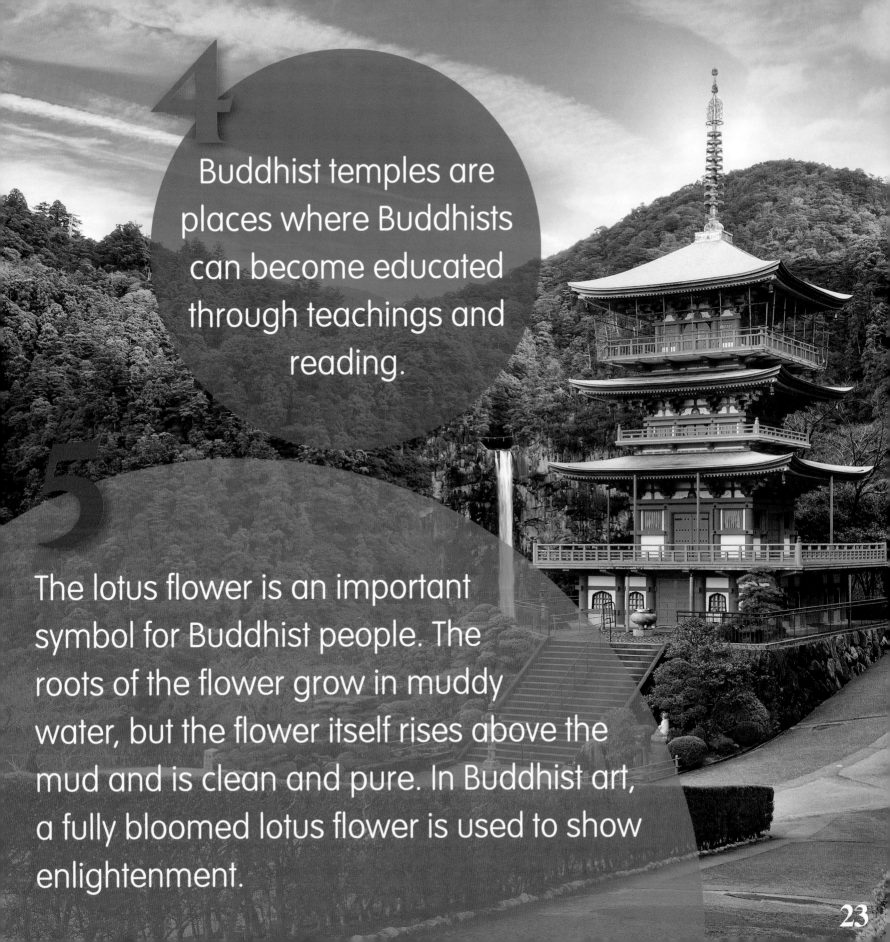

4 Buddhist temples are places where Buddhists can become educated through teachings and reading.

5 The lotus flower is an important symbol for Buddhist people. The roots of the flower grow in muddy water, but the flower itself rises above the mud and is clean and pure. In Buddhist art, a fully bloomed lotus flower is used to show enlightenment.

GLOSSARY

chant to repeat a word or phrase over and over again

contents everything that is within something

festivals when people come together to celebrate special events or times of the year

meditating a religious act where a person thinks calm thoughts

reborn to be born again

shelter protection against something

shrine a place of worship

suffering to feel pain or experience something unpleasant

worship to show respect for a god or gods